DREAM TREEHOUSES

extraordinary designs from concept to completion

Alain Laurens | Daniel Dufour | Ghislain André | La Cabane Perchée

Text by Sonia Buchard
Preface by Daniel Herrero

Photographs by Jacques Delacroix
Illustrations by Daniel Dufour

Translated from the French by Zachary R. Townsend

ABRAMS, NEW YORK

CONTENTS

40

ARLENA DI
CASTRO / TUSCANY / ITALY

Luxury in the wild

46

CALVADOS / FRANCE

The treehouse and
the beech tree

52

VAUCLUSE / FRANCE

The little oak that
dreamed of a
treehouse

58

LYONS-LA-FORÊT /
CALVADOS / FRANCE

A spa in the trees

64

MERANO / HAUT-ADIGE / ITALY

A honeymoon suite
among the pines

100

STYRIA / AUSTRIA

A forest lookout tower

104

SARTHE / FRANCE

The treehouse that
does the splits

108

BONNIEUX / VAUCLUSE /
FRANCE

A house in harmony
with nature

112

LOIR-ET-CHER / FRANCE

A modern
hunter's hideout

118

VAUCLUSE / FRANCE

A shelter for
squirrels

152

CALVADOS / FRANCE

The serpent of
Asclepius

156

SAVOIE / FRANCE

A fort in the sky

160

CHOLET / MAINE-ET-
LOIRE / FRANCE

The cabin of the egrets

164

GENEVA / SWITZERLAND

The baron's house

168

LA CROIX-VALMER /
VAR / FRANCE

An elevated
vacation destination

202

VAUCLUSE / FRANCE

A floating room

208

ARQUENNES / HAINAUT /
BELGIUM

A castle in the trees

214

LAKE GENEVA /
SWITZERLAND

The lookout on
the lake

222

PARIS AND GARD / FRANCE

The traveling
lighthouse

228

PROJECT / MEXICO

A treehouse among
the stars

Ah, let's dream!

I am a terrible poet, but I am speaking to all those who love what is beautiful and ephemeral, and who accept, as possible, new and extraordinary things, and celebrate them. These are the only things that interest me and occupy my days. It's important to understand that to me, dreams are more important than reality.

One day, a group of men arrived in my snail garden: friends of the springtime, artists of the treetops, and brothers of beautiful plants. They inhaled the scent of the earth, talked with the trees in the garden, tasted the mischievous breezes, and sat together as humble countrymen to talk.

A short while later, they sculpted puzzle pieces from the grain of a sacred tree that became a cabin of dreams! This cabin, made of beautiful wood that smelled of the tree's roots, was carefully installed in, and entrusted to, a sturdy tree, and thus it became a veritable "nest of dreams," simplistic in design—roof and walls, table and bed. Today, this cabin serves as a true escape from the rest of the world. Here, in the dim light of a small lamp, fragments of the outer world appear resplendent.

In this tree, feathered friends coo and chirp and then, at night, cross in a swarm across a vast sky of red clouds. Gentle rains quietly hum outside the cabin's windows and even heavy downpours seem innocent, as here one rests peacefully!

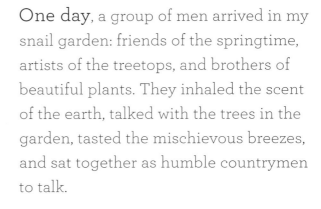

Up high, even the winter cannot bite at your legs or your fingertips, as the cold air is caressed and softened by contact with the warm wood.

In the cozy space of this cabin, the universe is larger, because here we walk through a world of daydreams: I have been in the middle of a scuffle with New Zealand's All Blacks rugby team as I aimed for the goalposts far in the horizon, all while smiling! I have met Geronimo on the run, encountered Amundsen the ice explorer, discovered a distraught gorilla in the mountains of Uganda, and even spent time with my mother in the comforting memories of my childhood.

A tree never reveals its secrets to the world. It relinquishes none of what it knows! It simply offers a delightful atmosphere of mystery. Peace reigns in the heart of its leaves, where the cabin rests.

Those who are part of La Cabane Perchée—Alain and Ghislain—have walked through various groves of trees and mountainous regions of the world and in all climates. And here and there— at the edge of a river, on the slope of a mountain, and at the end of a meadow— they have left behind their works of art, unique pieces that do the heart good and that embark the soul into a field of dreams and imaginary voyages where, without a doubt, it is the happiest.

So let's ascend upward . . . and dream in the world above!

—Daniel Herrero

A place of peace

W hat if all you had to do was climb a tree to gain a new perspective? Like Professor Keating, who suggested that his students stand on their desktops to see the world from a different angle in *Dead Poets Society*, Søren dreamed of building a neutral and calming space that would invite those who entered into it to consider the world in a different way. A specialist in conflict negotiation in Denmark known for solving the most difficult of disagreements, Søren transformed a former seaside hotel on the eastern coast into a reception center for both companies and individuals looking for tranquility. Every detail has been carefully thought out to create an atmosphere conducive to peace and relaxation. But serenity of space is not always enough to calm the spirit. The answer to this problem appeared when his sister, Christine, heard of a French company that built treehouses.

TREE VARIETY: **Beech**

HEIGHT: **26 ft. (8 m)**

INTERIOR AREA: **108 sq. ft. (10 m²)**

TERRACE AREA: **108 sq. ft. (10 m²)**

USES: **Mediation room and guest room**

WEBSITE: **www.kalovigcenter.dk**

Sheltered in the great beech tree and hidden from sight, the treehouse awaits its guests.

After Søren made a short visit to the Luberon, he decided to build a one-hundred-and-eight-square-foot (ten-square-meter) treehouse in the big beech tree in front of the center. As usual, it was created in the workshop of La Cabane Perchée then assembled on site like a Lego set, without cutting a single branch or putting any nails in the tree. After installation, the treehouse looked as if it had always been there. Appearing as a ring encircling the tree, it invites you to gaze on the beauty of the branches while giving the garden a distinct personality. Twenty-six feet (eight meters) above the ground, the interior space has been designed to comfortably accommodate working sessions for four or five people. From season to season, it seems that the great beech tree breathes consensus and respect into even the most stubborn of its guests.

The meeting table where conflicts are resolved.

To rise above everything, climb into the trees.

A moment of relaxation on the terrace, in the shade of the big tree.

The magnificent frame in red cedar.

A bridge over the jungle

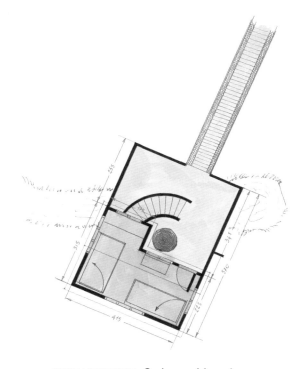

TREE VARIETIES: **Cedar and beech**

HEIGHTS: **33 ft. and 48 ft. (10 m and 15 m)**

INTERIOR AREA: **100 sq. ft. (9 m²)**

TERRACE AREAS: **108 sq. ft. and 132 sq. ft. (10 m² and 12 m²)**

UPPER DECK AREA: **79 sq. ft. (7 m²)**

USE: **Observation tower**

E ach treehouse is a childhood dream come true. For a little adventurer who, even after reaching adulthood, never gave up his wish to live high above the ground, this treehouse is a dream realized. Now a business leader wearing a suit and tie every Monday through Friday, the former Indiana-Jones-at-heart still imagines climbing trees in search of lost childhood experiences. On this large property, situated a few miles from Pontoise, flows a stream that has created a dangerous ravine. The treehouse, located in a great cedar tree with a footbridge suspended thirty-three feet (ten meters) above the ground and a terrace and upper deck in the neighboring beech tree, all within a lovely park in the Île-de-France, has transformed this area into a fantastic playground for the fearless, both young and old.

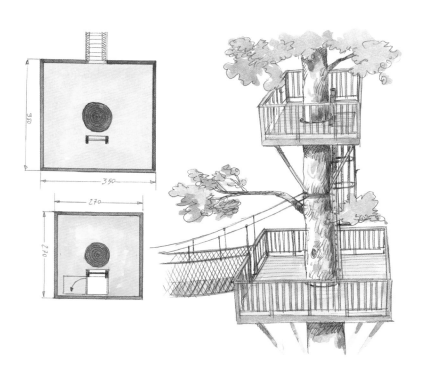

Views from the ground of the footbridge
encourage visitors to make the climb.

Beware of vertigo!

Even in high winds, the footbridge
remains perfectly secure.

Thanks to electricity, guests enjoy high-end comfort.

The realization of this structure was truly a technical feat and demanded all of Ghislain's expertise as carpenter to ensure it remained balanced at such a great height. The ascent of the spiral staircase that soars up the majestic conifer has become a rite of passage between the real world and the realm of the imagination. Arriving on the terrace, which is supported by glued laminated beams of red cedar, only the brave cross the bridge that hangs by metal cables and whose decking is made of treated Carolina pine. At thirty-three feet (ten meters) above the stream, if the wind picks up, each step is a rush of emotion! A covered section provides access to a second terrace that leads to the upper deck located about sixteen feet (five meters) higher. From here, you can admire the garden from a new perspective—and watch others climbing freely like leopards through the trees! On descent, the comfortably furnished treehouse offers a refuge where dreamers can recover from an afternoon, a night, or a weekend of their emotion-filled adventures among the trees.

The footbridge leads to a peaceful world.

A lawn chair invites you to sit and soak up the magic of the suspended terrace.

Marie's dacha

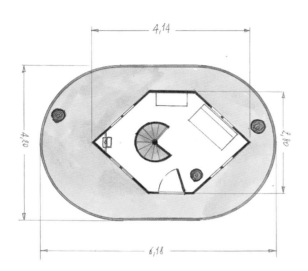

Little boys are not the only ones who want to live in the trees. In Moscow, the lovely Marie was nostalgic for her summer vacations spent among the branches. When she learned that a "somewhat-crazy" French team builds treehouses, she brought them into her big garden situated adjacent to a forest and asked them to create one for her. But there was no tree on the property that could bear the weight of a treehouse, no matter how small, so the team decided to create a structure built on stilts, hidden in the middle of a grove of three Douglas firs. This configuration would easily allow the platform to be positioned between the trunks. However, Marie was determined that a section of a tree be part of the interior, as if it had grown through the floor and roof. Fortunately, the trunk of one of the Douglas firs was perfectly straight, ensuring a tight fit through the roof without compromising the weatherproofing.

The semitrailer containing the construction materials arrived in the Luberon during winter, and the team began work in –22°F (–30°C) temperatures, first building the structure that houses a spiral staircase, then the platform, and finally the red-cedar cabin. Marie was able to spend the following spring happily decorating her secret garden. She began by painting the interior white, then adding cushions, curtains, lighting, and several accessories. In the summer, green plants and scarlet-red geraniums were planted in large planters, and the very next fall she was able to use her antique wood-burning stove and enjoy special moments of calm and serenity.

TREE VARIETY: **Douglas fir**

HEIGHT: **16 ft. (5 m)**

INTERIOR AREA: **129 sq. ft. (12 m²)**

TERRACE AREA: **198 sq. ft. (18 m²)**

USE: **Relaxing getaway**

You forget about the stilts and the
treehouse seems suspended in air.

Each owner furnishes her treehouse
as she sees fit.

The decorative stove also provides
ample heat in the winter.

The curved terrace overlooks the garden.

Everything inside is painted white.

The treehouse, the ultimate private space.

The cozy interior offers an escape.

A reader's retreat

I nside the treehouse, amid the quiet rustling of the trees, time seems to stand still. Each person organizes his life as he sees fit inside this wooden cocoon, without the concern of what others might think. Only essential or personal objects are brought in. When the owner of this property wanted to offer her husband a treehouse for his birthday, she immediately knew he would stock it with books, a comfortable sofa, and a reading lamp so he could spend hours immersed in his favorite novels. The bookcases, always imagined as part of the interior, were designed by Pierre, the team's joiner.

But, as always, the challenge was figuring out how to support the house in the trees! The large, lopsided oak did not seem big enough to support the weight of the many books, so a tree just a few yards away was called upon for assistance. The solution involved balancing the load between support points to ensure stability of the entire structure without cutting off a single branch or driving a single nail into the trunks.

TREE VARIETY: **Oak**
HEIGHT: **20 ft. (6 m)**
INTERIOR AREA: **75 sq. ft. (7 m²)**
TERRACE AREA: **113 sq. ft. (11 m²)**
USES: **Library and resting area**

Like a huge wooden kite, the terrace appears to float in the air.

The windows are double glazed for better insulation.

Viewed from the ground, the terrace and the stairs become sculptures that blend into the surrounding landscape.

A magnificent curved terrace had to be supported by glued laminated beams joined together a few feet below with rubber metal clamps. The structure is actually supported by a dual system of cables hanging from the branches and by supports that are connected to the main trunk. The covered section that allows access to the terrace gives way to a staircase that elegantly circles the first oak and leads up to the platform. Finally, the treehouse is wired for many reading lights—and a kettle for tea!

Details of the roof and the furnishings were completed by the joiners in the workshop.

A restaurant in a plane tree

Each tree has its own history, and you must take the time to listen to it. Trees are witnesses to a place's past, and the oldest preserve within them thousands of secrets heard over the centuries. At the heart of the Luberon, in a beautiful space that was transformed into a luxury hotel, a majestic plane tree stands, since the beginning of the seventeenth century, as an observer over olive groves and lavender fields. Its branches, which appear to touch the sky, command a silent respect just from their mere presence. While seated in the shade of the tree, Alain immediately realized how to adorn this giant using a circular design that would nest in the hollow of its huge limbs. The terrace, designed by Daniel, was immediately approved by the owner who saw the opportunity to reconnect with childhood memories while offering customers an exceptional experience that would take them back in time.

Taking measurements was difficult and the design process was slow. The task required courage and know-how to successfully build the structure without using stilts or even the smallest connectors. When the last planks were assembled—without ever touching the trunk and showing immense respect for the venerable

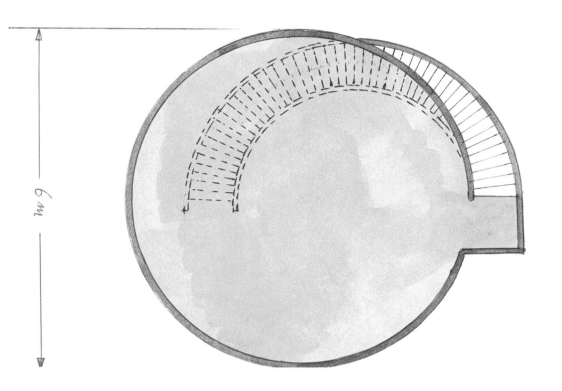

6 m

TREE VARIETY: **Plane**
HEIGHT: **23 ft. (7 m)**
TERRACE AREA: **301 sq. ft. (28 m²)**
USE: **Lunch or dinner in a tree**
WEBSITE: **www.andeols.com**

At night, the monumental staircase lights
up like hundreds of small fireflies.

The terrace was designed to withstand a weight of more than sixty-two pounds per square foot (300 kg/m²).

tree—the result was even more spectacular than expected. In the summer or winter, this "wooden crown" pays tribute to the branches without being a hindrance to the tree. The wide staircase, designed to facilitate the needs of the service staff, embraces the colossal trunk and provides access to a shaded terrace where the branches spring from the floor like geysers. Customers who are lucky enough to get a table at this popular venue have a rare experience while nestled in the privacy of the tree. At night, by the candlelight and LED lighting that accentuates the curve of the stairs, some say they have heard the tree reveal its secrets.

A simple terrace or a work of art?

The architecture of the treehouse honors the
four-hundred-year-old plane tree.

Alain Laurens
Founder of La Cabane Perchée

Luxury in the wild

TREE VARIETY: Umbrella pine
HEIGHT: 23 ft. (7 m)
INTERIOR AREA: 452 sq. ft. (42 m²)
TERRACE AREA: 431 sq. ft. (40 m²)
USE: Bed-and-breakfast
WEBSITE: www.lapiantata.it

Tarzan and Jane no longer have the exclusive right to life in the trees. Men and women no longer sleep among the branches of trees to protect themselves from wild beasts, but instead to return to a life close to nature and in harmony with the elements. For the managers of this beautiful Tuscan property converted into a bed-and-breakfast, the ultimate experience in luxury provides an escape from the everyday by providing relaxation among the lavender fields with the comforts of a five-star hotel. But to realize this lofty dream, La Cabane Perchée had to design a solid structure built on stilts that was capable of withstanding the weight of a treehouse measuring over eight hundred square feet (eighty square meters), as well as withstanding the strong winds at the top of the hill. The large umbrella pine extends its arm over the roof in a protective gesture. The roof is painted black to contrast with the colors of the sky, the olive grove, and the lavender fields.

With a view of the swimming pool below, the interior leaves no comfort forgotten, and its design was entrusted to interior decorator Claudia Pelizzari. For this combination of glass, steel, and cedar, she imagined a sophisticated interior with attention to every detail: LED lighting; heating and air conditioning; and a Corian shower, a crystal headboard, and a home theater—proving there is definitely no need to choose between luxury and a life in the wild!

There is an illusion of transparency thanks to the terrace's glass railings originally envisioned by the owners.

The terrace is like a raft, floating on a sea of olive trees.

The treehouse has all the comforts of a five-star hotel, including its glass shower.

The interior architecture by Claudia Pelizzari contains numerous high-quality materials.

The treehouse and the beech tree

TREE VARIETY: **Beech**

HEIGHT: **30 ft. (9 m)**

INTERIOR AREA: **144 sq. ft. (13 m²)**

TERRACE AREA: **215 sq. ft. (20 m²)**

USE: **Family gathering place**

Some trees seem destined to serve as shelters for treehouses. As if they have patiently waited their turn, their branches grow decade after decade in such a way as to better accommodate a treehouse when the time comes. History doesn't reveal if Louis-Philippe's minister of education, who acquired the land of this former Cistercian abbey, dreamed of building treehouses. Perhaps the idea crossed his mind as he was planting local and rare species of trees such as chestnut, hornbeam, wild cherry, Lebanon cedar, giant sequoia, thuja, and Austrian pines on both sides of the small valley.

Nearly two centuries later, these trees have become the gems of this park, and many of the minister's successors dreamed of building treehouses. After surveying the vast property, which includes five acres (two hectares) of woods and one hundred and seventy-three acres (seventy hectares) of grassland, a huge two-hundred-year-old beech tree with deep roots was unanimously chosen. But even though the tree's stature was ideal for a treehouse, the task was still daunting. It required renting a lift truck to take accurate measurements and to closely observe how the limbs interlocked. This colossal tree gave the builders a lesson in humility, but it eventually accepted the lovely angular treehouse. These days, the tree and its treehouse are visited regularly by mobs of young people who undertake ascending its magnificent swirling staircase to spend a few hours in the arms of the treehouse and the beech tree, away from everything else.

The treehouse looks tiny
in the big tree.

You can stay at the treehouse year-round,
thanks to its well-insulated construction.

The trunk and branches surround the little house like tentacles.

At thirty feet (nine meters) tall, the enormous tree, with its huge branches, demands respect.

The shaded terrace is a cool escape in hot weather.

The staircase ascends to a
dizzying height.

An incomparable artist,
an appreciation for
others, a good friend

Daniel Dufour
Cabin concepts

The little oak that dreamed of a treehouse

The word cabin comes from the Latin *capanna*, which means "that which contains only one standing man." In other words, a small, cramped space, designed to accommodate only the basics. So a tiny shack measuring sixty square feet (about six square meters) was built in this little oak tree, whose frail stature could never have supported more weight. There was a large cedar tree located just a short distance away that was considered, but it was not approved, so the little oak tree was to be the only option in which to realize the owner's childhood dream.

Still, the construction of this treehouse was only possible thanks to the light weight of the wood used, which came from a red cedar specially imported from Canada. This extremely rigid and imputrescible precious wood is four times less dense than other woods. Pink in color, it turns gray over time, taking on the color of the oak tree's trunk and blending in when surrounded by foliage.

TREE VARIETY: **Oak**

HEIGHT: **12 ft. (4 m)**

INTERIOR AREA: **60 sq. ft. (6 m²)**

TERRACE AREA: **100 sq. ft. (9 m²)**

USE: **Getting back to basics**

The art of simple living in the heart of Provence.

Although ideal for light and sturdy treehouses, western red cedar is very acidic and causes ferrous metals to rust, which requires the use of stainless-steel screws.

The terrace at nap time.

The red cedar's characteristic odor, which disappears after the second year and naturally repels insects and eliminates microbes and fungi, comes from its oils. Thanks to the strength of this ubiquitous North American tree variety, the little oak tree was able to bear the weight of the cabin on its shoulders, like Atlas, with the help of discreet glued laminated beams that join together on its lower branches. Inside is a bed with drawers, four casement windows, and beach chairs where visitors can relax while admiring the mountain views. Sometimes happiness is that simple.

In the tiny interior, the large bed and mosquito netting take visitors into a dreamlike state.

A spa in the trees

TREE VARIETY: **Pine**

HEIGHT: **15 ft. (5 m)**

INTERIOR AREA: **135 sq. ft. (13 m²)**

TERRACE AREA: **65 sq. ft. (6 m²)**

USE: **Massage room**

WEBSITE: **www.hotel-licorne.com**

Even at just fifteen feet (about five meters) above the ground, the world is perceived differently. In the confined space of a small treehouse located between the branches of a tree, the senses are alert to the sounds of nature, the scent of bark, and the movement of the leaves. Breathing becomes slower and conversations take place in low voices, as if to not disturb the birds. In the heart of a Normandy beech grove, customers of a luxury hotel experience these sensations in the massage room built on stilts overlooking the pool and garden. After climbing a few stairs, they enter a bright and warm room where they are soon to receive treatments. But they are often surprised to find that the magic of their experiences begins even before the first touch of the masseuses' hands, as they become aware of the reassuring presence of the tree. The big pine—with its slender silhouette that shields the treehouse from the sun and rain like an elegant natural umbrella—creates a deeply relaxing atmosphere inside its timber enclosure. Gazing at the branches through the large picture window and letting oneself be charmed by the song of a titmouse, those who enter here suddenly feel swept far, far away.

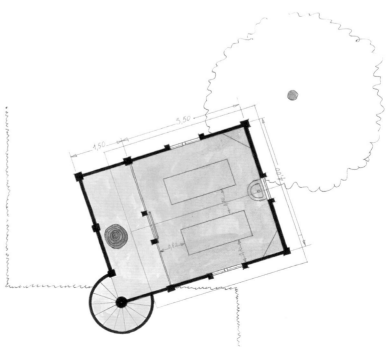

The treehouse creates a calm atmosphere
that guests appreciate.

In summer, open windows let in a gentle breeze.

The architecture echoes the wooden farmhouses and slate roofs of the region.

Spa treatments take place to the sound
of leaves rustling in the breeze.

The pine doesn't support the structure's
weight but still offers its branches as shelter.

A man of careful planning, talent, and humor

Ghislain André
Partner, fellow carpenter, and workshop director

A honeymoon suite among the pines

TREE VARIETY: **Pine**

HEIGHT: **23 ft. (7 m)**

INTERIOR AREA: **377 sq. ft. (35 m²)**

TERRACE AREA: **700 sq. ft. (65 m²)**

USE: **Hotel suite**

WEBSITE: **www.hotel-irma.com**

The definition of what is romantic has evolved. Just as shepherdesses long ago dreamed of marrying handsome princes and living in golden palaces, today, young women dream of special hiding places where they can snuggle with their loves. In the Haut-Adige, hoteliers who were in the constant pursuit of perfection wanted to offer their customers an exceptional place where they could drift off gazing up at the Milky Way while listening to the sound of the breeze and be awakened by singing birds. A grove of resinous trees located just over one hundred and sixty feet (forty-nine meters) from the main building on the hillside seemed an ideal place to build luxury suites perched in the trees.

Again, Ghislain had to design a structure built on stilts, accessible by a winding staircase, that would house a fully equipped suite weighing more than thirteen tons (twelve metric tonnes)! Several plans were proposed, and as soon as they were finalized, the entire treehouse was built in sections in the workshops at Saint-Saturnin-lès-Apt before being assembled and mounted on site. The water hoses and sewer connection, as well as the electrical cables, were carefully hidden inside one of the stilts, keeping them completely concealed. In the interior, which opens up to the branches of the pines, lovers enjoy all the comforts of a hotel suite. And if the weather permits, a simple move allows the large bed, which is adjacent to the window, to be pulled out onto the terrace for sleeping under the stars.

The comfort level is up to par with high-end hotels.

The eave of the roof is notched to make room for the pine's trunk.

The very spacious terrace overlooks the hotel pool.

The bed was designed to slide easily
onto the terrace.

The cozy nest at night.

The glow of lights twinkling between the branches creates a magical atmosphere.

A haven for nature lovers, nestled between trees and mountains.

The suspended kingdom

At age five, a little boy was not dreaming of a treehouse, but of a castle where he could be a knight. His younger sister dreamed of a princess's castle where she could draw, and his big brother of a place to spend time devoted to his passions. And since nothing was more important to their father than his children's dreams, he had a treehouse built for each of them, situated between conifers and birch trees near their residence northeast of Moscow. The oldest had a split-level treehouse with skylights that were controlled by remote, the middle child had a lovely treehouse accessed by a climbing wall, and the youngest had a fortress equipped with swings. The three houses were connected by red-cedar footbridges so that the three children and their friends could visit one another without ever stepping a foot on the ground.

For the record, building the children's dream quickly became a nightmare for La Cabane Perchée. The semitrailers holding the building materials were detained in Vilnius, Lithuania, for several weeks, and the team had to wait for customs to release them before the cargo finally reached the city of Tver. The construction lasted two and a half months, during which two teams, those of Thomas and Ghislain, took turns constructing five treehouses, including the three little gems for the children, each with its own unique identity. The kingdom suspended between the trees was finally completed, and when the siblings took possession of them, their joy immediately made everyone forget about all of the difficulties, giving way to the magic of childhood.

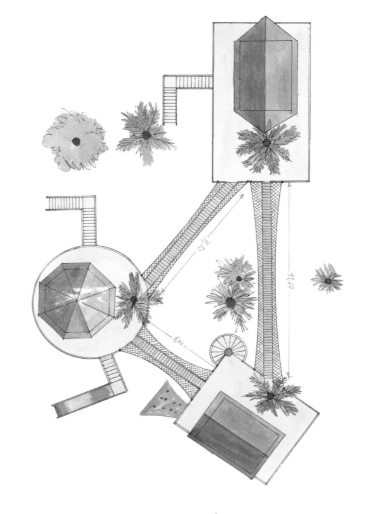

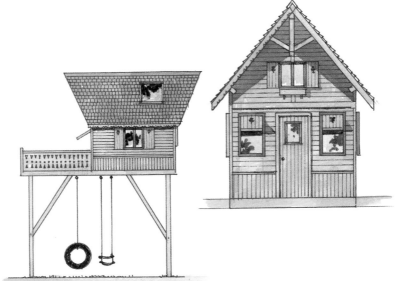

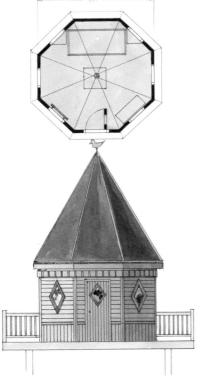

HEIGHTS: **16 ft. (5 m)**

INTERIOR AREAS: **183 sq. ft., 188 sq. ft., and 183 sq. ft. (17 m², 18 m², and 17 m²)**

TERRACE AREAS: **420 sq. ft., 237 sq. ft., and 172 sq. ft. (39 m², 22 m², and 16 m²)**

USE: **Children's rooms**

A keep replaced the originally planned
hexagonal tower.

The footbridges were constructed with
seven-foot (two-meter) sections in red cedar.

*A children's playground in the
heart of the Russian countryside.*

Long footbridges flex slightly
with each step.

In the foreground, a climbing wall offers an adventurous way to access one of the treehouses.

Each cabin has a different entry; here, a beautiful spiral staircase provides access.

A hot bath at -22°F (-30°C)

In the north, when a blanket of snow covers the forest and nature becomes hostile, we must invent a new way of enjoying life outdoors. Millennia ago, by simply combining wood, fire, and water, the Scandinavians developed an intense relaxation technique that wonderfully soothes both sore bodies and minds: the Swedish bath. Using a red-cedar barrel filled with water from the river, a wood stove crackling with fragrant logs from surrounding conifers, and water heated to 102°F (39°C), well-being is assured. Within minutes, the muscles relax, the body's toxins evaporate along with life's worries, and stress dissipates into the cold air.

Once the three children were content with their treehouses (see page 70), their father decided to build a space for adults. An imposing wooden structure on stilts was thus designed, providing a large terrace, a huge well-insulated room, and a beautiful bathroom. But the real architectural challenge was creating a terrace that was strong enough to support a Swedish bath weighing almost three tons (two and a half metric tonnes)! In the workshop, the design team combined their creative efforts to inconspicuously reinforce the structure by using a system of trestles and glued laminated beams made of Douglas fir and larch.

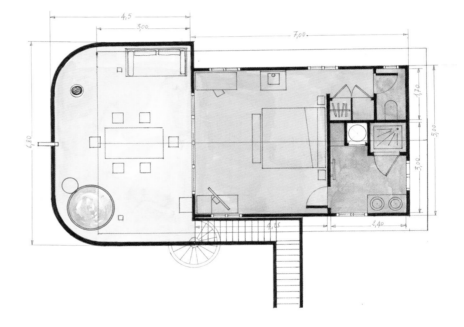

HEIGHT: **20 ft. (6 m)**

INTERIOR AREA: **398 sq. ft. (37 m²)**

TERRACE AREA: **194 sq. ft. (18 m²)**

USE: **Swedish bath house**

The Swedish bath offers stunning views of the Volga and the fishing cabin.

The wooden structure was designed to support both the cabin and the Swedish bath, which weighs several tons.

From the cabin, perched on its long legs, visitors can see far into the distance.

Hot mineral-bath therapy between the branches: a moment of pure pleasure.

During the second year, the color of the red cedar fades.

After a long construction period, the cabin was thoughtfully furnished and the Swedish bath was installed, filled, and heated, making it an inviting retreat even when the temperatures dip well below freezing. And today, while the children play, the adults submerge themselves in the rejuvenating water and savor the pleasures of living in Russia while looking out toward the Volga.

A fishing lodge on the Volga

Before flowing into the Caspian Sea, the Volga crosses the vastness of the Russian plains, inspiring artists and poets with each of its twists and turns. At its source a few miles downstream of the Valdai plateau, the wide river is a paradise for pike fishing. To make each fishing trip a moment of pure pleasure, this nature lover imagined building a cabin in the midst of this river.

INTERIOR AREA: **188 sq. ft. (18 m²)**
TERRACE AREA: **452 sq. ft. (42 m²)**
USE: **Fishing**

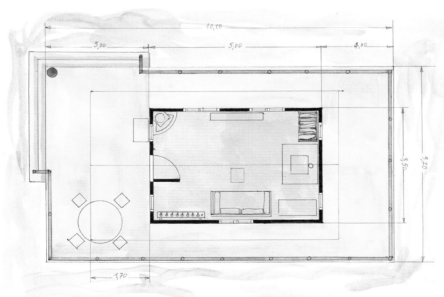

Daniel designed a spacious platform above the water, a beautiful arched roof covered with copper tiles that gleam in the sun, and a warm interior with a wood stove and a rack for fishing rods. The technical team designed the concrete platforms on which the structure would be tied down, taking care to replace traditional aluminum floaters with polypropylene ones that can withstand the onslaught of ice that arrives with the long Russian winters.

Once the cabin was complete (and not without some difficulties), Alain was invited to visit just before Christmas. To his surprise, he saw his hosts literally walking on the water in front of him. Even if the ice had melted slightly in the sun, its thickness made the icy crossing safe. And what a joy to admire the spectacle of the frozen Volga at sunset before retiring to warm up by the fireplace!

The rounded copper tiles shimmer at sunset.

An island retreat in the Volga River.

In the shape of an inverted hull, the ceiling of the floating cabin takes on the appearance of a fishing boat.

The reflection of the amber-colored roof in the frozen
river contrasts with the harmonious grays of the sky.

The golden eagle suite

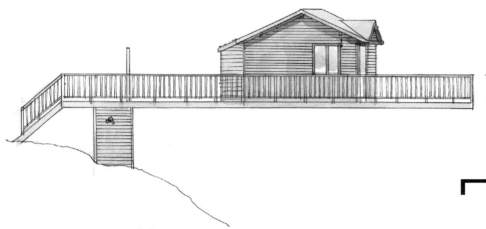

TREE VARIETY: **Oak**

HEIGHT: **24 ft. (7 m)**

INTERIOR AREA: **309 sq. ft. (29 m²)**

TERRACE AREA: **420 sq. ft. (39 m²)**

USE: **Hotel suite**

WEBSITE: **www.primland.com**

The beauty of a treehouse lies not only in the tree that cradles it, but also in the surrounding landscape. In the eastern United States, the Blue Ridge Mountains were a perfect setting for a treehouse. In the fall, when thousands of trees are red-orange and the ridge is covered with a bluish haze, the beauty is breathtaking. This provided a great opportunity to be invited to a magnificent resort to design an amazing suite in the trees!

The morning of their initial visit, Alain and Daniel went in search of the perfect tree on the grounds of this vast area. But after hours of walking, they returned to the hotel unsuccessful, confused about not being able to find the perfect place that would provide both a sufficiently strong tree and an interesting view of the mountains. They resumed their search the next day and finally found a beautiful oak tree that overlooks a sheer drop of more than nine hundred feet (two hundred and seventy-four meters). Using watercolor, Daniel sketched the project, including a ramp, a large rounded terrace overlooking the valley, and a spacious interior with a bedroom, corner living room, and bathroom.

Back in the studio, Ghislain and his team began building the treehouse in separate pieces, and a few weeks later, embarked on a voyage across the Atlantic. The entire team arrived to assemble the pieces directly above the ridge, where guests can live the American dream in the magical landscape of the Appalachians.

The Golden Eagle suite in the Blue Ridge
Mountains sits on the edge of the blue horizon.

The treehouse boasts top-quality finishes and decorative flourishes.

A luxurious treehouse in the Appalachians.

Just under the terrace, the cliff drops
nine hundred feet (274 meters).

A serious, rigorous man
with a big heart

Thomas Dupérier
La Cabane Perchée assembler

Between the blackbird and the hornet

By building his house between the branches of a tree, man imposes on the territory of birds, squirrels, and insects. And after a few days away, he realizes that they have taken over his premises, leaving small piles of acorns here and there. The design of the treehouse must be in tune with nature and show the utmost discretion if the structure is to be accepted by the tree and its ecosystem.

In the gardens of an old converted farmhouse in Geneva, a first sketch was drafted for a particular oak tree before we noticed that a colony of hornets had already settled there, dangerously hollowing out its trunk. As a consequence, another oak was chosen at the back of the property for the wonderful view it offered of the topiary garden and the Alps. The first proposal was to create a pentagon-shaped terrace and an angled house around the two main limbs. The interior was to be divided into two parts: a corner constructed into a sleeping alcove and an office. But after talking with the owner, who was a talented architect, the project evolved into a circular design with a large crescent-shaped room overlooking a curved terrace through a large, curved picture window encircling the trunk of the tree. During construction, a blackbird built its nest in the frame, confirming that the tree's inhabitants accepted the project!

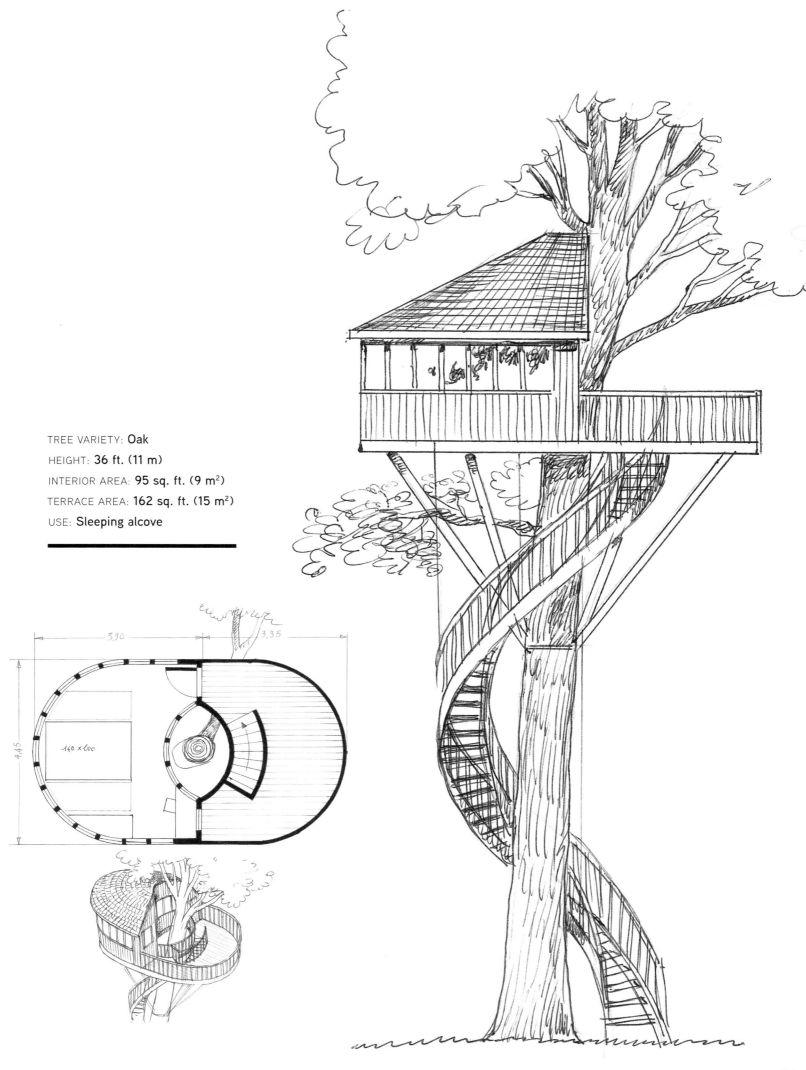

TREE VARIETY: **Oak**

HEIGHT: **36 ft. (11 m)**

INTERIOR AREA: **95 sq. ft. (9 m²)**

TERRACE AREA: **162 sq. ft. (15 m²)**

USE: **Sleeping alcove**

3,90

3,35

4,45

140 x 200

The curves of the treehouse contrast with the rectilinear shapes of the topiaries.

Placed in front of a curved window, the bed
occupies nearly the entire space.

*Without the ability to fly like birds,
man takes pleasure in nesting in the
trees a few days out of the year.*

As always, the view from the terrace
determines the position of the treehouse.

A forest lookout tower

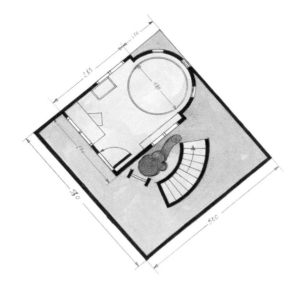

TREE VARIETY: **Oak**

HEIGHT: **33 ft. (10 m)**

INTERIOR AREA: **104 sq. ft. (10 m²)**

TERRACE AREA: **129 sq. ft. (12 m²)**

USE: **Writing nook**

F rom thirty-three feet (ten meters) high, the landscape is completely reimagined. Even a well-known environment can be full of surprises—the perception of distance and space changes, and what is hidden at ground level is suddenly visible. On this property located on the borders of Austria, Slovenia, and Hungary, a large oak tree grows atop a bluff towering over a wooded valley. Its location made it an ideal tree in which to build a treehouse for a family's three children.

In the first sketches, the treehouse, facing the border and topped with a second higher level, resembled a lookout tower. A protected ladder would have allowed the children to climb onto the upper level located forty-six feet (fourteen meters) above the ground to watch the deer grazing below. The project, however, was not to be realized, as the sixty steps leading to the terrace provide a sufficient height for an impressive view. The design of this staircase was a challenge for the team, which had to take the slope

The less straight the trunk, the farther away the spiral staircase must be from the central axis.

The view from the terrace
over the forest below.

Often children's treehouses are eventually taken over by their parents.

and the twisting trunk into account so that the curve could slide in between the branches of the tree while also fitting between connectors that support the structure and rest on a rubber metal collar located ten feet (three meters) below. But at this height, despite the support, it is common for treehouses to sway a little if there is wind!

Even though the original designs provided many amenities for the children, their mother ultimately took possession of the treehouse and gradually transformed it into an office. Today, the children have abandoned it, and it is now their parents who ascend the staircase to admire the landscape and to be absorbed in the tranquility of the forest.

With each step, the small valley and hills change perspective.

The treehouse that does the splits

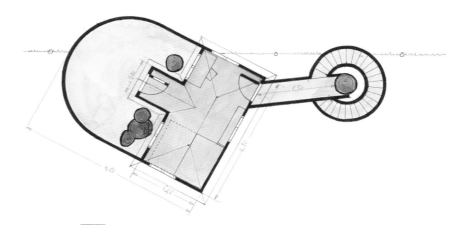

TREE VARIETY: **Oak**

HEIGHT: **36 ft. (11 m)**

INTERIOR AREA: **113 sq. ft. (11 m²)**

TERRACE AREA: **140 sq. ft. (13 m²)**

USES: **Observing and sleeping**

In the art of building treehouses, as with any art, constraints foster creativity. A twisted trunk, a sloping ground, or too close or too distant trees are obstacles imposed by nature that require treehouse builders to seek out innovative solutions. On the edge of the Sarthe, the owner of a beautiful mansion dreamed of building a house in one of the one-hundred-year-old oak trees on his land to observe the animals in the surrounding countryside. From Daniel's first sketches, one of the trees was selected to support the weight of the treehouse by a system of connectors and collars, while another was called upon to support a spiral staircase that twists twice around its trunk up to thirty-six feet (eleven meters). When possible, having the staircase on a separate tree from the house is ideal, because it allows for more useable space on the terrace, which does not have to accommodate the entrance to the stairs.

The sections were designed and cut out in the workshop, but the carpenters had the foresight to consider several options for securing the treehouse at its planned height. Once on site, the assembly team had to make some modifications by securing the platform to both trunks using special horizontal planks, giving the treehouse its originality!

A unique construction perched
between two trees.

Suspended in air, this little treehouse defies the laws of gravity.

A well-arranged interior, where every square foot is used thoughtfully.

The bench, which transforms into a bed, was created by the workshop joiners.

A house in harmony with nature

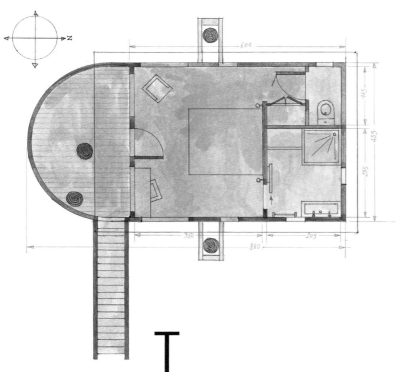

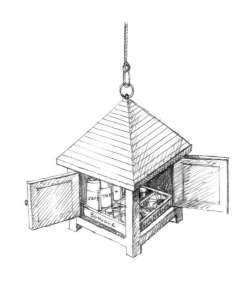

In recent years, sleeping in trees has become a symbol of a lifestyle in harmony with nature. Many people look for a new balance in life through environmentally friendly activities as they become aware of the excesses of society and the need to change their habits. Mass tourism has given way to a desire for simplicity and authenticity without giving up pleasure, comfort, or beauty.

This guest room was designed to meet all the expectations of this new type of tourism by offering the chance to be immersed in unspoiled countryside. Situated on a thirty-seven-acre (fifteen-hectare) property with truffle oak, lavender, cherry, pine, and olive trees, the treehouse's weight is balanced between four pine trees and two stilts.

TREE VARIETY: **Pine**

HEIGHT: **13 ft. (4 m)**

INTERIOR AREA: **280 sq. ft. (26 m²)**

TERRACE AREA: **118 sq. ft. (11 m²)**

USE: **Guest room**

WEBSITE: **www.maisonvalvert.com**

The treehouse consists of a large terrace overlooking the mountains of the Petit Luberon, a bright bedroom, a bathroom, and a private toilet.

Here, luxury is discreet: recessed lighting in the eaves of the roof and contemporary sconces provide soft lighting. The decor is elegant without being ostentatious. While air conditioning can be turned on during periods of extreme heat, it doesn't take away from the seductive serenity of this place, situated between heaven and earth. Little by little, nature reasserts itself. The sun marks the passing of time and the rest of the world seems to disappear behind the horizon.

Everything is designed for a feeling of comfort and well-being inside the wooden cocoon.

Giving comfort a new meaning.

In the moonlight . . .

A bathroom worthy of a luxury hotel.

The breeze lifts the treehouse's curtains.

A modern hunter's hideout

TREE VARIETY: **Oak**

HEIGHT: **23 ft. (7 m)**

INTERIOR AREA: **118 sq. ft. (11 m²)**

TERRACE AREA: **291 sq. ft. (27 m²)**

USE: **Wildlife observation deck**

Historically, hunters have built treehouses in the forest to observe animals without being seen. Serving as places of observation and escape, a treehouse's relatively basic method of construction has become symbolic of a lifestyle that combines simplicity with respect for nature. In Sologne, where hunting is a long tradition, a landowner cleared a large area in a cornfield to attract deer and wild boar. To study their behavior without disturbing them, he envisioned building a shelter twenty-three feet (seven meters) high, at the intersection of two forest roads. But the two trees selected were located twenty feet (six meters) apart, so a stilt had to be erected on the edge of the road as a third support for the platform. Installed to span the road, the triangular layout has evenly distributed weight, because of the twenty-six-foot (eight-meter) beam, which was secured underneath by angular brackets. Cables that provide opposing force were installed to ensure safety of the structure.

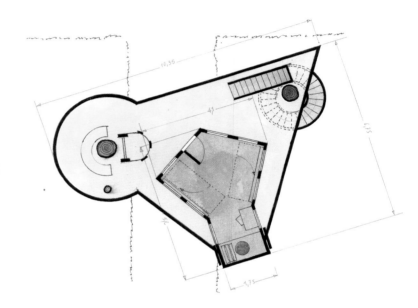

Overlooking the roadway, the treehouse lets
farm equipment pass.

The treehouse was designed to
accommodate two people.

The upper deck, a round table on the terrace,
and a wood stove were not installed as planned,
but this lovely, rustic furnished treehouse has
no less charm.

Naps are more pleasant in the shade
of an oak tree.

*The art of seeing without
being seen.*

An ideal vantage point for watching wild game in any season.

Accuracy,
refinement,
and laughter

Pierre Nègre
Joiner

A shelter for squirrels

Like squirrels that build their nests in trees as shelter, children take refuge in a treehouse.
Even if the treehouses are tiny in size, children feel at home in a place where they can make their own rules. This owner from the Luberon built a treehouse high in an oak tree for his grandchildren so they could enjoy the same small wonders that he experienced as a child. The chosen tree, located at the edge of a stone retaining wall, is sturdy but small. Its short stature made the usual system of connectors impossible, so we had to build the structure on two wide beams suspended by cables hanging from the upper branches. To ensure the stability of the structure, two stilts were added, one of which supports the spiral staircase that leads directly into the treehouse, where children can cross to reach the small terrace overlooking the stone wall. The roofing shingles made of red cedar, the detailing on the roof trim, and the attention to finishing touches make this simple treehouse a perfect little nest to welcome the children's summer adventures.

TREE VARIETY: Oak
HEIGHT: 10 ft. (3 m)
INTERIOR AREA: 86 sq. ft. (8 m²)
TERRACE AREA: 65 sq. ft. (6 m²)
USE: Children's playhouse

The oak was transformed into a
playground for children.

A picnic on the terrace.

During summer vacation, this little treehouse is filled with toys and books.

Outfitted with a table, a comfortable bed, and picnic supplies, the treehouse is a fun setting for summer adventures.

The hut in the purple beech

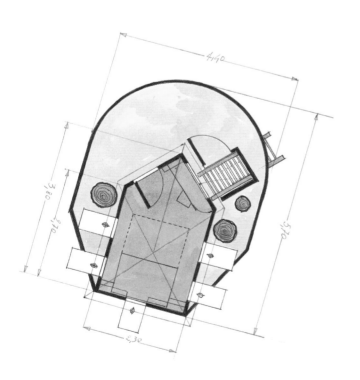

Majestic and intimidating, two-hundred-year-old trees sometimes seem to challenge treehouse designers. Amid the twists of their thick branches, no space seems capable of accommodating a structure of any kind. It's always a great temptation to cut one or two limbs to make room, or even to do a little pruning to clear a spot for a staircase, but trees should be treated with an infinite amount of respect. And builders should take the time to study the trees' sizes and be creative in their approach to erecting a treehouse in their dense foliage.

TREE VARIETY: **Purple beech**
HEIGHT: **25 ft. (8 m)**
INTERIOR AREA: **79 sq. ft. (7 m²)**
TERRACE AREA: **113 sq. ft. (11 m²)**
USE: **Lake views**

123

Numerous windows allow you to enjoy the view of the lake.

At the edge of Lake Geneva, the magnificent purple beech that dominates the shore has long been a spot preserved for the many species of birds that live on the lake or arrive on stopovers during migration. When a nature lover decided to establish his resting spot here too, the project seemed futile at first. But a structure with a few square feet of living space located twenty-five feet (eight meters) above the ground eventually took shape. After a week of construction, the purple beech tree welcomed a new resident, whose presence was made as unobtrusive as possible.

After climbing the rungs of the protected ladder, a small break on the terrace is welcome.

During the fall, the scenery changes dramatically when the trees are adorned with brightly colored foliage.

Concerto for a plane tree

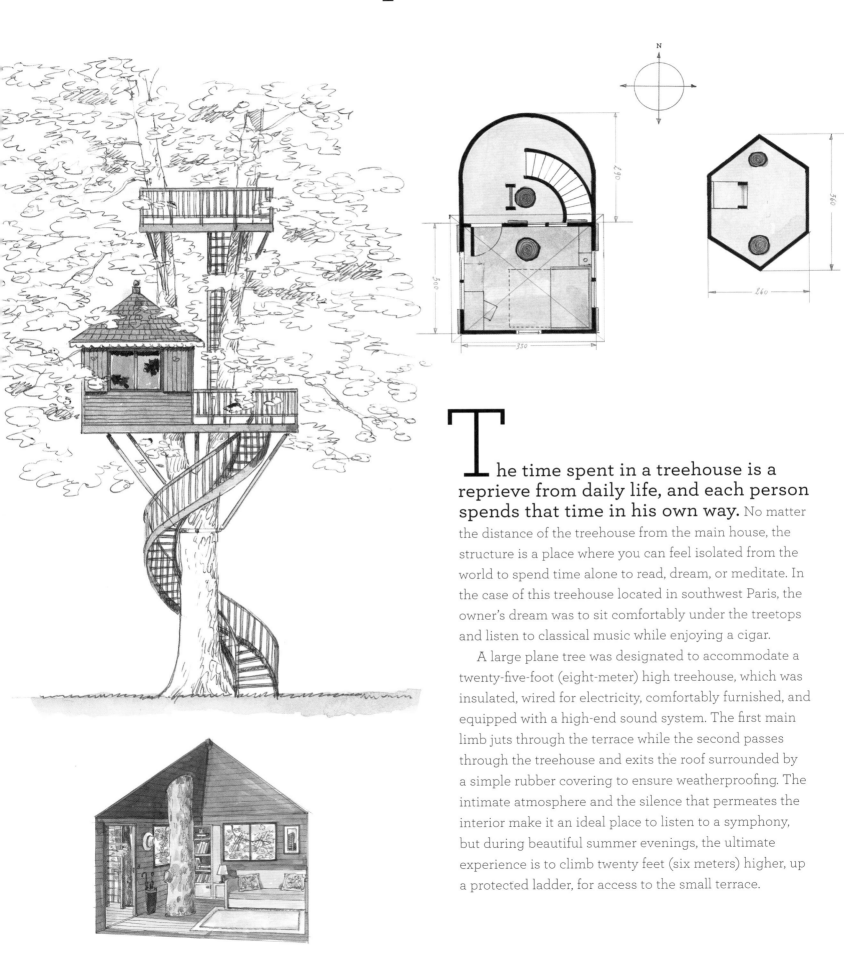

The time spent in a treehouse is a reprieve from daily life, and each person spends that time in his own way. No matter the distance of the treehouse from the main house, the structure is a place where you can feel isolated from the world to spend time alone to read, dream, or meditate. In the case of this treehouse located in southwest Paris, the owner's dream was to sit comfortably under the treetops and listen to classical music while enjoying a cigar.

A large plane tree was designated to accommodate a twenty-five-foot (eight-meter) high treehouse, which was insulated, wired for electricity, comfortably furnished, and equipped with a high-end sound system. The first main limb juts through the terrace while the second passes through the treehouse and exits the roof surrounded by a simple rubber covering to ensure weatherproofing. The intimate atmosphere and the silence that permeates the interior make it an ideal place to listen to a symphony, but during beautiful summer evenings, the ultimate experience is to climb twenty feet (six meters) higher, up a protected ladder, for access to the small terrace.

TREE VARIETY: **Plane**

HEIGHTS: **25 ft. and 44 ft. (8 m and 13 m)**

INTERIOR AREA: **95 sq. ft. (9 m²)**

TERRACE AREA: **65 sq. ft. (6 m²)**

HIGH TERRACE AREA: **67 sq. ft. (6 m²)**

USES: **Cigar and music room**

In summer, the music terrace is completely hidden by the foliage.

The rough bark of the plane tree is invited in and becomes a decorative element.

A pulley to bring up some provisions for after the concert.

Here, protected by the foliage, the owner, and music lover, has installed a plush sofa and weather-resistant high-tech speakers whose wires are camouflaged against the trunk. Under the starry sky, when the first refrains of an opera resound from under the branches, it's as if even crickets hold their breath to not miss a single note.

An outdoor concert hall, forty-four feet (thirteen meters) high.

The interior showcases a careful attention
to decorative details.

Competence,
attention to detail,
and a gentle
approach

Aimé Barré
Carpenter

Room service, treehouse style

Many people living in urban areas feel the urgent need to recapture the simplicity of an arboreal life. In order to satisfy their desire for nature, peace, and frugality, one couple decided to retire to a family estate in the Loire Valley and build two guest houses in oak trees. In the first treehouse (see the second on page 160), there are very memorable details. After ascending the great oak to twenty-seven feet (just over eight meters) in height, taking in the panorama of the surrounding countryside, spotting a deer running through the trees, organizing their belongings in the lighted room, then testing the large bed, guests make their way out onto the terrace where they discover the pulley system located on the other side of the trunk.

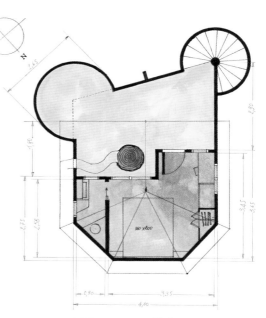

TREE VARIETY: **Oak**

HEIGHT: **27 ft. (8 m)**

INTERIOR AREA: **118 sq. ft. (11 m²)**

TERRACE AREA: **129 sq. ft. (12 m²)**

USE: **Guest room**

WEBSITE: **www.bernardiere.com**

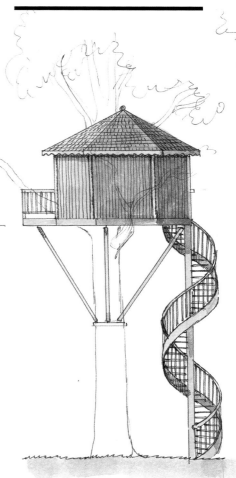

The staircase ascends from the flowers
growing at the base of the trees.

On the terrace, a guest can commune
with the great oak.

From the inside, there is a wide-angle
view of nature.

With just a few pulls of the rope, guests
can raise the small basket that delivers their
lunch, which they can enjoy under an awning
in the silence of the woods. By operating this
amusing, old pulley (which was obtained from
a second-hand store), visitors are engaging in
an old-fashioned method that seems straight
out of a storybook. The world in which it takes
just a single click to shop online has suddenly
vanished, giving way to the one where you
simply pull a rope to retrieve a meal. Each
time they discover an aperitif or some food for
breakfast in their basket, guests experience a
feeling of lightness and freedom as they are
reminded of the physical distance between
them and the ground.

A vacation in harmony with nature.

135

The maple tree chalet

If overcoming obstacles requires imagination, then some structures offer real brainteasers. A narrow grove of fifteen tree trunks required a concentrated effort to figure out how to wind through them to build a suspended structure. In front of a beautiful chalet of a posh resort in the Swiss Alps, this unprecedented situation resulted in a keyhole-shaped plan: a hexagon leading to a small hallway that opens up to a tiny, round furnished room with a circular bench. Once the challenge of the design and connectors was solved, a solution for the roof had to be found. This was solved by using spruce shingles, which allowed a more complex shape than the typical red-cedar shingles—it is not easy to connect a straight roof to a round roof. Finally, special attention was paid to the finishing touches of the interior and exterior designs, which were inspired by the typical architecture of a chalet. Even in the winter, the owners can take refuge in this adorable treehouse, light the wood-burning stove, and enjoy the view.

TREE VARIETY: **Maple**

HEIGHT: **15 ft. (5 m)**

INTERIOR AREA: **57 sq. ft. (5 m²)**

TERRACE AREA: **102 sq. ft. (10 m²)**

USE: **Tea room**

4,20

3,00

1,65

4,00

1,50

In winter, after lighting the stove, the small room is comfortably heated.

Building in this narrow grove was a challenge.

The cozy treehouse offers a unique view of the snow-capped peaks.

A night in the mountains in a perfectly
secluded treehouse.

An orchard retreat

N°3

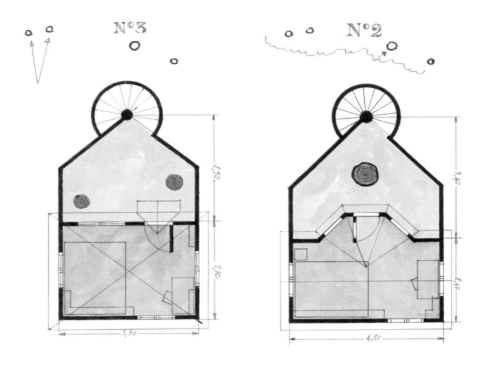

N°3

N°2

Neither in the city nor quite in the countryside, the gardens around Paris can offer the best of both worlds. Roughly nine miles (fourteen and a half kilometers) from Paris, this treehouse is maintained by an artist who is passionate about nature and plants, and who has created a little secret haven among the trees. Next to the large family home, the owner built this little treehouse near an apple orchard in search of inspiration and tranquility. The layout selected boasts a staircase that twists around an oak tree and leads to a sixteen-foot-long (five-meter-long) walkway, which offers stunning views of apples growing on a trellis, with Parisian rooftops and the Eiffel Tower in the background. In the summer, the garden terrace is a great place for lunch, to have a drink, or just to daydream.

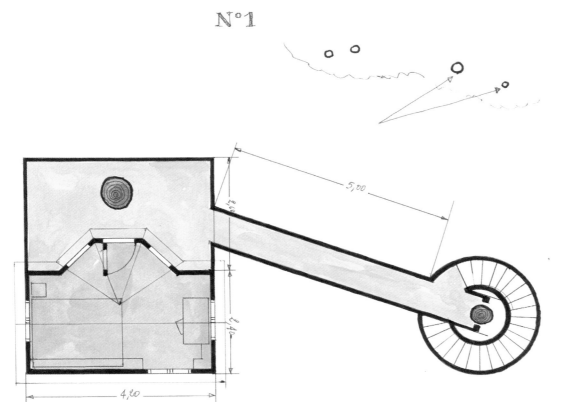

5,00

4,20

TREE VARIETY: **Oak**
HEIGHT: **20 ft. (6 m)**
INTERIOR AREA: **112 sq. ft. (10 m²)**
TERRACE AREA: **96 sq. ft. (9 m²)**
USE: **An escape from city life**

Nº1

The roof shingles and exterior siding are made of red cedar.

Sitting among the branches of the apple orchard makes thoughts of the city seem like distant memories.

The pulley is a must-have accessory to obtain a refreshing summer drink.

The large double-glazed window opens the treehouse to the outside.

The interior, perfectly insulated by large aluminum windows, reflects the personality of its owner. The works of artist Katharina Leutert (paintings on wood depicting the feathers of Jivaro warriors) adorn the walls, while the inviting motif of cushions and light creates a cozy and comfortable atmosphere. The bench, made at the workshop by Pierre, transforms into a bed to accommodate guests.

The treehouse is entirely devoted to introspection and meditation, but the owner also wished to create another dream treehouse—a garden shed on the ground floor. Here, she can store gardening tools and arrange apples on racks, all the while forgetting the presence of the nearby city.

. . . and in the garden below, the apple cabin keeps you grounded.

An improvised garden sculpture.

A dream cabin for the garden.

The workshop joiners were tasked with building the interior furnishings.

Reliability,
curiosity, and a
musical accent

Marius Piquet
Joiner

The serpent of Asclepius

TREE VARIETY: **Oak**

HEIGHT: **23 ft. (7 m)**

INTERIOR AREA: **97 sq. ft. (9 m²)**

TERRACE AREA: **75 sq. ft. (7 m²)**

USE: **Painting studio**

In Greek mythology, Asclepius, son of Apollo and god of medicine, is always depicted with a serpent wrapped tightly around a staff.

Was the serpent—a symbol of the earth and the renewal of life, and which is represented on the caduceus of doctors and pharmacists—the inspiration for this long staircase that embraces the oak? The stairs also seem to hug the trunk like the serpent from the Garden of Eden in Genesis. But no matter the inspiration, it adorns the silhouette of the tree and leads to a small sun terrace where a tree limb snakes between the guardrails.

To create this languid shape, Ghislain and Aimé, the workshop's experts on staircases, used 3-D computer software to create the exact shape of each piece. The vertical nature of the oak allowed them to position the steps very snugly with the trunk, giving the illusion that the staircase wraps around the tree.

265

210

185

375

260

340

The spiral staircase winds around the tree.

Treehouses are always designed to face the best view.

The interior has been designed as an artist's studio, with large windows and a large working surface.

The large oak easily carries the weight of the treehouse.

The pieces were then constructed by alternating sheets of wood with layers of glue in a custom mold, which was held together by clamps for two days. Once dried and removed from the mold, the shape was refined by hand and assembled on site.

Two months later, when the owner requested several changes to the entrance to the terrace from the staircase, the team was able to reconstruct the new pieces using the computer software and replaced the top steps without impacting the rest of the treehouse.

A breathtakingly high ascent.

A fort in the sky

TREE VARIETY: **Larch**

HEIGHT: **7 ft. (2 m)**

INTERIOR AREA: **70 sq. ft. (7 m²)**

TERRACE AREA: **108 sq. ft. (10 m²)**

USE: **Children's room**

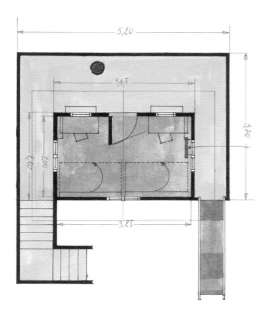

W hether made with boxes in the living room, with bed covers, or with a blanket hanging between two chairs in the garden, childhood forts make lasting memories. Starting as early as preschool, children love to make their own worlds to play "grown-up" in safe and familiar environments. And before you know it, they are building their forts in their grandparents' garden, isolated from the rest of the adult world, with or without their grandparents' help.

To please his twin granddaughters, a generous businessman built them a miniature replica of his chalet in Savoie, placing it on stilts. The architectural details were reproduced identically, including the motifs in the shutters and along the railings, and those of the frieze along the eave of the roof. On the edge of the garden, this adorable playhouse is joined to larch trees. One emerges through the floor of the terrace, much to the delight of the twins. The interior has been converted into a game room, with two desks for playing and drawing, and two sofa beds for resting. After riding the slide down to the ground, the twins can sway on swings under the deck.

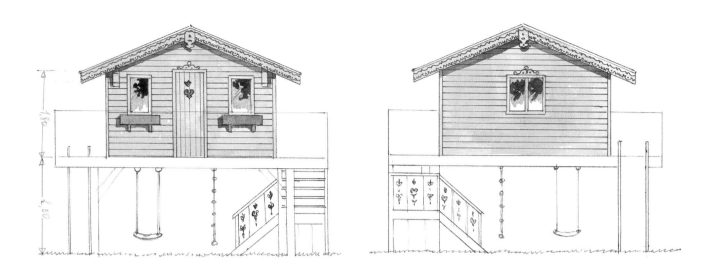

157

A dusting of snow on the railing of the miniature chalet.

A space built for imagination and games.

This treehouse seems like the setting of a story by Hans Christian Andersen.

While envisioned on the opposite side of the treehouse in the initial concepts, in the final design, the staircase was built next to the slide.

The quaint atmosphere of an all-wood treehouse.

The cabin of the egrets

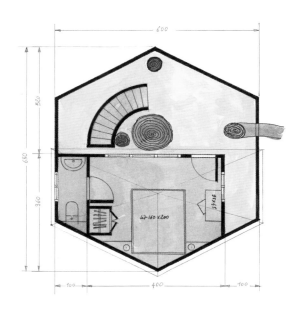

Surrounded by majestic oak trees, a country road leads to a pond where herons, egrets, and ducks take roost. Here, a second treehouse was constructed to serve as a guest room on this family's land in the Loire Valley (see the first on page 132). Daniel chose a beautiful oak tree, nearly two hundred and fifty years old, for its elegant silhouette and its ideal location in front of the water.

But before deciding how to place a platform more than three hundred square feet (twenty-eight square meters) between the tree's limbs without distorting the tree or cutting any of its branches, it was necessary to take several measurements and carefully study how to best position the treehouse. The staircase, built in the workshop using glued laminated beams, consists of thirty-two steps that lead to a pointed terrace where the thick trunk and the three main limbs leave just enough room to place two chairs in the sun. Inside, the room is comfortably furnished, but without a single pretension. Dry toilets, a round sink, and a small cistern of water make up the bathroom. Candlelight preserves the rustic atmosphere that makes life in the trees so magical.

TREE VARIETY: **Oak**

HEIGHT: **20 ft. (6 m)**

INTERIOR AREA: **154 sq. ft. (14 m²)**

TERRACE AREA: **172 sq. ft. (16 m²)**

USE: **Guest room**

WEBSITE: **www.bernardiere.com**

At night, you can hear the sound of frogs
in the neighboring pond.

Peering through the branches of the tree, you can watch the fish jump in the water.

Morning visitors.

The stunning scenery of the pond and the garden can be seen through every window.

The baron's house

TREE VARIETY: **Oak**

HEIGHT: **30 ft. (9 m)**

INTERIOR AREA: **108 sq. ft. (10 m²)**

TERRACE AREA: **129 sq. ft. (12 m²)**

USE: **An escape from the real world**

At the age of twelve, Côme Laverse du Rondeau climbs a tree to escape having to eat a plate of escargots and decides to never come down. Demonstrating strength of character and an exceptional stubbornness, the hero of the novel *The Baron in the Trees* by Italo Calvino spends his life walking from tree to tree giving his contemporaries an extraordinary lesson in freedom and eloquence, because, as he states, "to see the world clearly, you have to look at it from a distance."

The adventures of the arboreal philosopher, who inspired the formation of the company La Cabane Perchée, motivated the team to give this treehouse in Geneva a long staircase that snakes between two oaks. The first steps wrap around a nearby trunk before reaching a footbridge that allows one to stop and gaze at the garden from sixteen feet (five meters) up. Then, a spiral staircase, supported by an attached post, extends upward to the great oak's highest limbs, which cross a small terrace. The three different levels invite you to enjoy the transition from the "lower world" to the "world of trees." In the way that Côme Laverse du Rondeau leaves behind the social constraints and mediocrity of the world on the ground to achieve his ideal state, the hosts of this treehouse leave their worries down at the foot of the stairs and ascend into a new world where they can sleep, write, relax, or meditate far from their peers, only to be troubled by the occasional visiting squirrel or bird.

After crossing the footbridge, there is a final climb up the spiral staircase to the terrace.

"Côme looked at the world from the top of the tree. Everything, seen from here, was different."

—Italo Calvino, *The Baron in the Trees*, 1957

Wooden casement windows are preferred in rustic treehouses.

A bed, a desk, candles, and several good books.

167

An elevated vacation destination

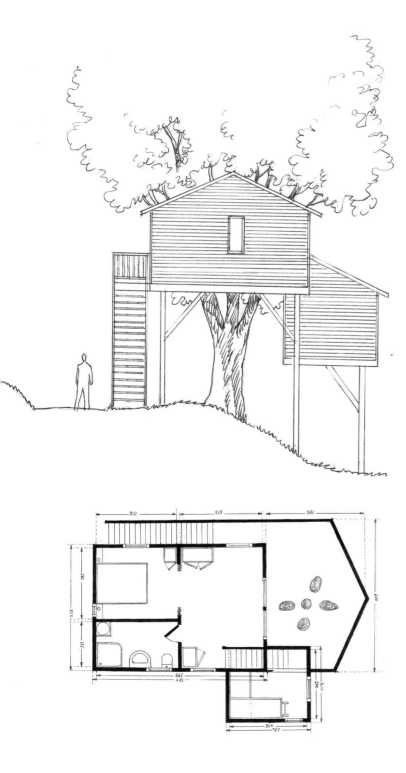

In a treehouse, you have the luxury of being alone or with only those you love. It can be a place of solitude or conversation, silence or shared laughter. Life in a treehouse intensifies the feelings of intimacy and human bonds. Just as they are for lovers, treehouses are also dreams for families—parents looking for a simple lifestyle in harmony with nature while their children live in a fantasy world, sheltered in their wooden cocoons.

On the French Riviera, the owners of a beautiful hotel nestled between vineyards, orchards, and rose gardens already offer couples the chance to be alone in a treehouse one hundred and seventy-two square feet (sixteen square meters) in a one-hundred-year-old oak tree. Faced with constant demands from parents with young children, they ordered a second treehouse to accommodate a family of four. In front of the vineyards, a huge oak seemed an ideal place to erect a large treehouse and a terrace on stilts, with a total area of more than five hundred square feet (over forty-six square meters)!

TREE VARIETY: **Oak**

HEIGHTS: **11 ft. and 19 ft. (3 m and 6 m)**

INTERIOR AREA: **382 sq. ft. (36 m²)**

TERRACE AREA: **198 sq. ft. (18 m²)**

USE: **Family guest room**

WEBSITE: **www.chateauvalmer.com**

A living area one hundred and forty square feet (thirteen square meters) gathers the entire family together.

A canopy covers the double bed in the master bedroom.

To preserve the privacy of each family member, Daniel designed a two-level space: the main level includes a living room, a bathroom with a bathtub, and a master bedroom. The second level, located below, is the children's room, accessible by a small internal staircase. Pierre created rustic furniture along with closets and bunk beds. In the shadow of the tree limbs, a spacious terrace overlooks the gardens, floating on a sea of greenery that emits the aromas of Provence—a true dream vacation!

A return to the basics.

The large treehouse is hidden by the foliage of the oak.

The children's room with bunk beds
and closets.

The warmth of the wood, the rustic but elegant
decorations: no detail is left unplanned.

An open mind, tenacity, and a smile

Zsolt Nyerges
Carpenter

A ship's bow

How do you successfully design a space in a small country garden that feels entirely remote and private? And how, in the midst of the Wallonia region in Belgium, do you succeed in creating a space that evokes the feeling of being in a foreign and exotic land? On this beautifully landscaped property, many varieties of aquatic plants bloom at the edge of a pond covered with water lilies. To take advantage of this unique environment, the idea to build a structure on large stilts, two of which would be anchored on solid ground and the other two in the water, was proposed. With this design, the large circular terrace juts above the water like the bow of a ship, giving the impression that it will slice through the waves and into the nearby sedges.

In the first sketches that Daniel created, the treehouse had a perfectly hexagonal layout, which would have emphasized its exotic appearance. But this configuration consumed too much space, so with agreement from the owner, a more conventional plan was proposed. The new plan added sixty-five square feet (six square meters) for a small kitchen and bathroom. Once completed, this lofted cabin, whose wide eaves suggest an Asian influence, totally transformed the garden. On some summer days, when spotting the treehouse through the leaves, you can imagine being in Thailand.

HEIGHT: **10 ft. (3 m)**
INTERIOR AREA: **199 sq. ft. (19 m²)**
TERRACE AREA: **301 sq. ft. (28 m²)**
USE: **A garden retreat**

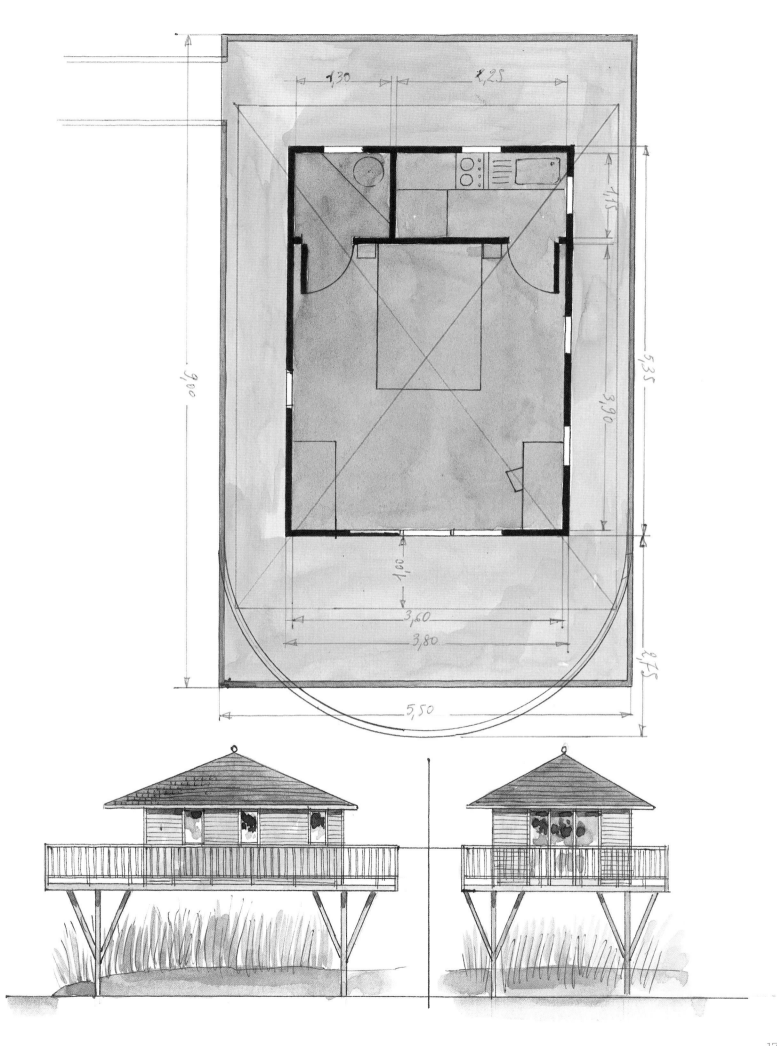

This treehouse was conceived as an oasis in the middle of the garden.

The circular terrace made of glued laminated
beams is entirely handmade.

The wide eave provides shade
for the walkway.

The treehouse is perched near
the pond among the sedges.

A refuge in a pine forest

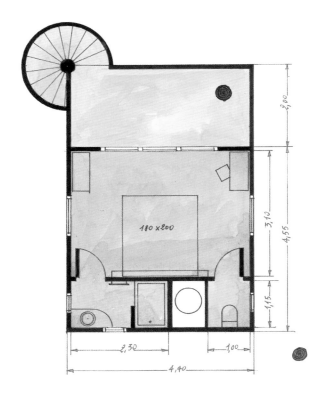

A treehouse can serve simply as a room separated from the rest of the house, a private space that allows one to escape the demands of family life or provides some independence for children, young couples, or visiting friends. At the heart of Provence, in a landscape worthy of Cézanne's paintings, a large farmhouse surrounded by pine and olive trees has been restored in a minimalist style to provide accommodations for a large family for the summer. Although they have a very spacious home that can accommodate many guests, the owners wanted to offer their friends the opportunity to spend the night in their own space on the far end of the property in a comfortable, furnished suite sixteen feet (five meters) off the ground.

For the first stage, the treehouse was built on three stilts, with a pine tree over thirty-three feet (ten meters) high acting as the fourth support. But the owners thought the height was too dangerous because the winds in the area can easily topple the largest trees.

TREE VARIETY: **Pine**
HEIGHT: **16 ft. (5 m)**
INTERIOR AREA: **194 sq. ft. (18 m²)**
TERRACE AREA: **97 sq. ft. (9 m²)**
USE: **Guest room**

The treehouse is planted firmly on its four
legs in the middle of the pine forest.

In the early morning, the view of the countryside is a true joy.

Consequently, two solid trestles were built to support the room, with the large pine tree in front playing a strictly decorative role, rising above the terrace to provide shade and some shelter. The spiral staircase wraps around an added post. Behind the large picture window, the treehouse has a beautiful room and an all-wood bathroom with a shower and heated towel rack. And in summer, the cicadas in the pine forest announce the arrival of morning.

An attractive bathroom, all in wood, is hidden behind the headboard.

The treehouse offers an intimate place where silence is disturbed only by the sound of cicadas.

An art deco watchtower

When designed as an extension of the tree that shelters it, a traditional treehouse is made entirely of wood. But when metal is introduced into the design, the result can be amazing, as in this treehouse built at the edge of a pool at a luxury hotel on the Balearic Islands. In the first draft of the design, the treehouse was to rest on stilts made of glued laminated larch beams. But the owners wanted to install towering picture windows that would have been extremely heavy and required oversized stilts. The idea then came to create a metallic structure whose elegant arabesque would take on the motif of the hotel's interior. The huge pine, in which the house is enveloped, plays a decorative role rather than a structural one.

TREE VARIETY: **Pine**

HEIGHT: **19 ft. (6 m)**

INTERIOR AREA: **194 sq. ft. (18 m²)**

TERRACE AREA: **82 sq. ft. (8 m²)**

USES: **Cocktails, dinners**

WEBSITE: **www.sonnet.es**

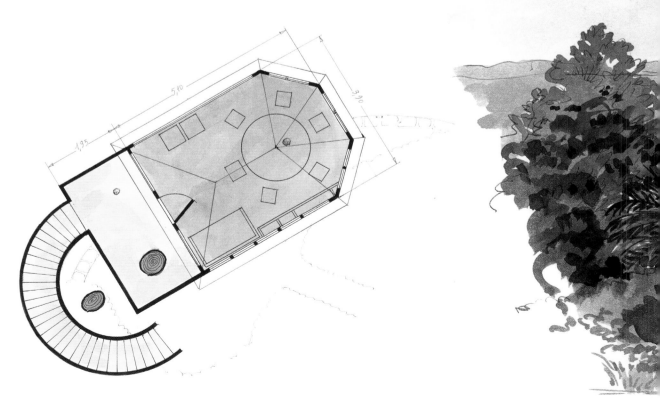

A unique view of the Serra de Tramuntana,
near Palma de Mallorca.

The treehouse that thinks it's the Eiffel tower.

Much more durable than wood, metal allowed the creation of ethereal supports that give the treehouse a distinct personality. The double-glazed windows could then be installed along with a large window that folds open. At sunset, guests ascend the semicircular staircase, arriving under a canopy that is crossed by the pine's limbs, then move to a table to enjoy a cocktail while admiring the rugged mountains of the Serra de Tramuntana. So chic!

The picture window folds closed at the first drop of rain.

The giraffe feeder

Building a place in the trees, man invites himself into the natural habitat of animals. But when the trees in question are huge and located in a giraffe exhibit in a zoo, he is confronted by more than the usual difficult questions! This was the challenge that La Cabane Perchée encountered when the owner of a zoo in Belgium wanted to erect an observation deck in his "African City" so that children could gaze eye to eye with its long-necked inhabitants. From the outset, taking measurements was an extremely delicate task. Huge plane trees up to thirty-three feet (ten meters) in height made it particularly difficult. Additionally, it was necessary to create a deck fifty-six feet (seventeen meters) long that could flex between the tree trunks and support the weight of dozens of families.

The project was designed by Daniel, Ghislain, and Aimé using their 3-D computer software to create a veritable carpenter's masterpiece whose technical complexity only experts could appreciate. The floor, sized and cut in the workshop, was made of treated Carolina pine and has a cue-stick shape—planks that radiate from the center, never the same length. At the end of the terrace, a staircase leads to the upper deck located twenty-six feet (eight meters) high and provides a view of the giraffe exhibit from above. The entire structure was mounted on stilts to meet all safety standards, and rails were drilled with irregularly shaped holes to resemble spots on a giraffe. The holes allow children to reach their hands out to feed leaves to the giraffes.

TREE VARIETY: **Plane**

HEIGHT: **26 ft. (8 m)**

TERRACE LENGTH: **56 ft. (17 m)**

USE: **Feeding giraffes**

WEBSITE: **www.pairidaiza.eu**

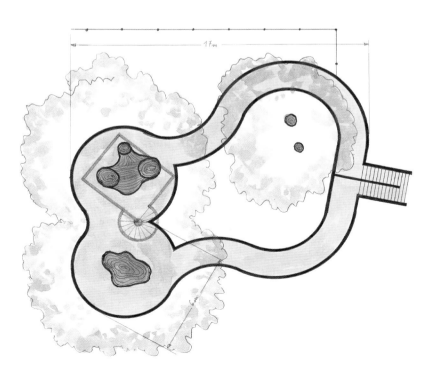

The cue-stick shaped floor is an attractive technical complexity.

A delightful face-to-face encounter with giraffes.

Giraffes come to eat delicacies that
visitors feed them.

A Chinese junk ship in the canopy

The feeling of being in a foreign land is not necessarily related to distance. For the owner of this zoo, located in the Wallonia region of Belgium, who has beautifully re-created the landscapes of the five continents, this fact seems quite true. It was therefore logical that he attempt to get away by building a treehouse in the huge trees of his "Chinese City," eliminating the need to cross the ocean. This was a very ambitious project that required building a duplex for two people, including a kitchen/dining room, a bathroom, and an upstairs bedroom—a small technical feat! The first level, topped with a hexagonal tower, rests completely on a platform suspended by cables hanging from the upper branches. The weight is shared among four one-hundred-year-old trees, with multiple cables and anchors used to evenly distribute the downward pressure. From the ground, the structure appears to float magically in the air. The interior has been finished with the same care as a luxury ship. Hidden ducts that mask the water supply, waste pipes, and electrical cables run along the tree. And every detail has been considered for maximum comfort. Even though this boat never sails, it nonetheless embarks passengers on an extraordinary voyage through the land of trees.

TREE VARIETIES: **Plane and beech**

HEIGHT: **36 ft. (11 m)**

INTERIOR AREA: **355 sq. ft. (33 m²)**

TERRACE AREA: **549 sq. ft. (51 m²)**

USE: **Voyaging away from the ordinary**

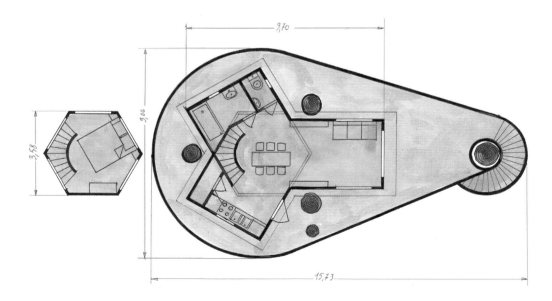

The structure is suspended by a cable system secured to the upper branches.

A floating terrace, or a Chinese junk ship situated between the branches?

The treehouse is integrated into the Asian theme of this part of the zoo.

The foliage in summer completely conceals the treehouse.

A floating room

In some places, nature seems to use all of its power to prevent people from spoiling it. In this corner of Provence, scrubland has taken over at the edge of a ravine thirty-three feet (ten meters) deep with a flowing stream. This steep section of a beautiful property has wild fig trees and one-hundred-year-old evergreen oak trees that amaze all those who venture here, but the land is not suitable for building, so only animals manage to inhabit the area. So how does one dare to build a treehouse suspended above the ravine as a surprise for the owner who is a well-known developer recognized around the world? The search for anchoring points required mobilizing many experts before digging holes several feet deep at the base of the cliff and filling them with a special cement to support the foundation. The wooden stilts that support the platform rest on highly resistant concrete pads located several feet below.

To access this treehouse, seemingly located at the end of the earth, a sixty-six-foot (twenty-meter) footbridge that is supported by a metal structure on the other bank was built from red cedar, selected for its extraordinarily light weight. On the terrace, two of the tree's limbs protrude through the structure as if trying to reclaim its territory.

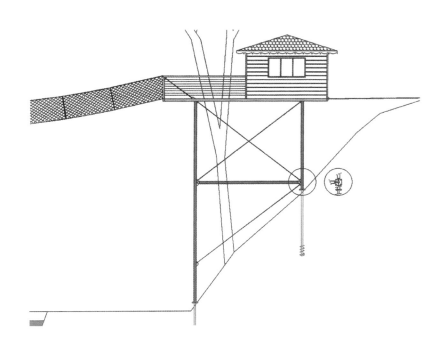

TREE VARIETY: **Evergreen oak**

HEIGHT: **33 ft. (10 m)**

INTERIOR AREA: **162 sq. ft. (15 m²)**

TERRACE AREA: **258 sq. ft. (24 m²)**

USE: **Living in harmony with nature**

Around the branches, space was left to let the tree grow over time.

A pleasant surprise waits for guests at the end of the footbridge…

The large picture windows open the treehouse to nature.

A footbridge sixty-six feet (twenty meters) in length makes even the most courageous visitor hesitate.

The destination makes crossing the long footbridge worthwhile.

Under the terrace, a precipice nearly
thirty-three feet (ten meters) deep.

The only way to access the terrace is
by crossing the steep ravine.

A castle in the trees

Choosing between the beauty of natural scenery and the comforts of a luxury hotel room can be difficult. However, the owners of a castle hotel, dating back to the seventeenth century and located south of Brussels, have built a treehouse in the vast park area of this property, paying as much attention to comfort as they do in the rooms of the hotel. After reaching the small wooded area by foot or bicycle, guests ascend a great curved oak staircase and arrive on a terrace just below the top of the majestic tree.

TREE VARIETY: **Oak**

HEIGHT: **20 ft. (6 m)**

INTERIOR AREA: **263 sq. ft. (24 m²)**

TERRACE AREA: **129 sq. ft. (12 m²)**

USE: **Guest room**

WEBSITE: **www.restauration-nouvelle.be/
_lescabanesdemarie/EN/**

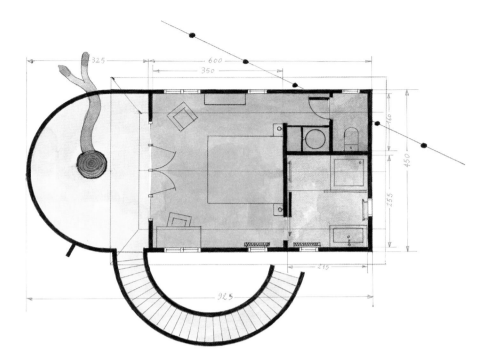

The treehouse is supported by
its beautiful oak.

Inside, they find many amenities prepared especially for them, including a mini bar, a fruit basket, a coffeemaker, and a champagne bucket. In the bathroom, where fluffy bathrobes are waiting, there is a walk-in shower alongside a large bathtub, and the toilets are separated by a partition. Guests can bask in one of the chairs on the terrace, sit at a small table to enjoy breakfast inside, or call for room service to deliver a hot dinner twenty feet (six meters) above the ground.

Whether in winter or summer, the experience seduces couples seeking romance—especially those who try the beautiful horse-drawn wooden carriage located at the other end of the park and managed with the same great care—and has them rushing to book another overnight stay!

There is even a bathroom
with a large bathtub.

No matter the season, one can enjoy the beauty and quiet of the woods.

The size of the room accommodates
a large bed.

The lookout on the lake

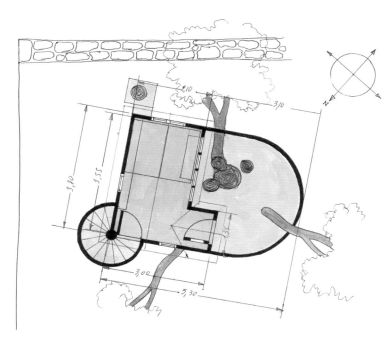

TREE VARIETY: **Oak**

HEIGHT: **26 ft. (8 m)**

INTERIOR AREA: **86 sq. ft. (8 m²)**

TERRACE AREA: **97 sq. ft. (9 m²)**

USE: **Meditation room**

A treehouse is a place that calls upon all five senses. Once high up, visitors often shift imperceptibly toward a more contemplative mood, an inner journey that brings back memories from childhood. On Lake Geneva, this treehouse was built in a large oak tree and stirs a range of feelings entirely different from those generated by the nearby house and garden. Climbing the steps of the spiral staircase, the gentle design of the wooden incline generates a sense of security and comfort. Once on the terrace, tree limbs spring from the floor to make their presence known, as if waiting to be admired and cherished. At twenty-six feet (eight meters) above the ground, the relationship with the tree is more intimate, more tangible.

Unlike its initial sketches, the staircase circumvents the small neighboring oak.

Climb twenty-six feet (eight meters) above the ground and see the lake from an unparalleled viewpoint.

The rounded terrace offers two views of the lake and garden.

Upon entering a small room that looks out onto the lake from a large picture window, the scent of wood instantly reminds you of the first forts you built during summer vacation when you were eight or nine years old. When it is windy, the sound of the creaking trees evokes the rustling of a boat's sail. The view of the lake and the Alps, already beautiful from the foot of the tree, is quite different when seen through the branches. Silence has a different sound inside the treehouse, solitude another feeling, and time another dimension. Perhaps this is why treehouses are magical places where dreams are born.

The curve of the staircase has become
a decorative element in itself.

A beacon of comfort and relaxation
at night.

The desire to learn, team spirit, and a love for race cars

Amaury Santi
Electrician/plumber

The traveling lighthouse

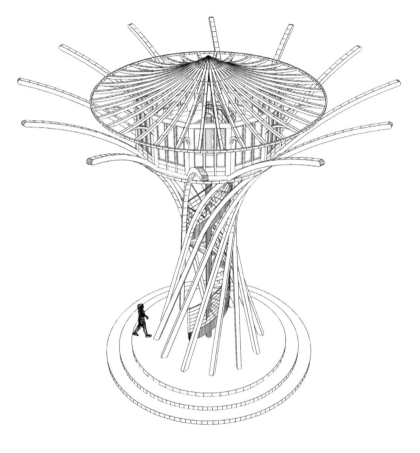

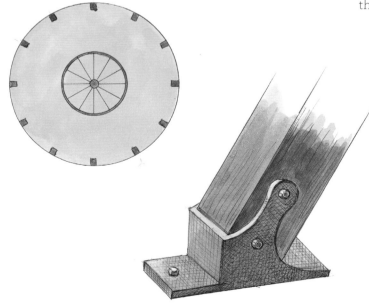

Creating a spectacular treehouse in record time on a concrete floor without even the slightest anchoring points while meeting strict safety standards is always a gamble. Arranged by the organizers of the 2013 "The Art of the Garden" exhibition show at the Grand Palais in Paris, the challenge seemed unachievable. But the technical conundrum amused Ghislain, who sketched out a project on his computer as if to push his limits as a designer. A majestic flower-shaped structure on which a circular treehouse topped with a Japanese-style roof was perched appeared on the screen. The design intrigued Nathalie and Paul Vranken, owners of Champagne Pommery, who financed its construction.

Several weeks later, the truck containing the pieces made in the workshop arrived early in the morning at the Grand Palais, a cathedral of glass and steel. The design team will never forget the four days and three nights of hellish construction that followed, including approvals for the construction and surreal technical constraints.

HEIGHT: **46 ft. (14 m)**
INTERIOR AREA: **75 sq. ft. (7 m²)**
USES: **Exhibition room and large sculpture**
CURRENT ADDRESS: **Domaine de Jarras,**
           Aigues-Mortes

This fully self-supporting structure is weighted
down by a platform filled with sandbags.

The cedar supports are composed of three parts, joined together by metal clamps.

From the glass roof of the Grand Palais to the landscape of the Camargue region, this treehouse was designed to shine like a jewel in the sky.

An hour before the official opening of the exhibition, in a buzzing atmosphere as exciting as it was frightening, the treehouse was finally completed with the application of the sponsor's logo forty-six feet (fourteen meters) above the ground. Visitors could not take their eyes off the rosewood structure that ascended toward the glass roof and sparked the urge to climb up it to admire the landscaped gardens from above (see the video at www.la-cabane-perchee.com). After three thousand five hundred climbs by guests, the treehouse was dismantled and parted to cross France by truck and to continue its life on the edge of the Jarras in Aigues-Mortes. Transformed into a monumental sculpture, it now shines brightly at dusk, continuing its destiny as an exceptional treehouse.

The lighting of the treehouse gives a new look at night.

Like a UFO in the Camargue night.

A treehouse among the stars

"Always aim for the moon, even if you miss, you'll land among the stars," wrote Oscar Wilde. After fifteen years of architectural challenges to construct treehouses around the world, the desire to reach for the stars remains. From the most modest to the most utopian, each realized childhood dream has pushed the boundaries of imagination and strengthened our desire to create exceptional places to live magical moments. The experience of the Grand Palais has shown that a lofty cabin can reach toward the heavens without necessarily relying on a tree. Why not imagine one that can stand independently on a sandy beach at the edge of a lagoon, or on top of a mountain, overlooking the landscape with elegance and discretion?

And why, says Ghislain, not imagine the comfort of absolute luxury with a huge, round picture window to observe a panorama of the sky from bed? And imagine still if the interior design combined simplicity of wood with high-end finishes worthy of the greatest hotels in the world? For the lazy, an elevator could replace the spiral staircase behind the wooden connectors, gently taking guests up to the suspended nest after taking a dip in the waves.

Today, that dream cabin is awaiting its time and a chance to be refined by La Cabane Perchée before, one day, becoming a reality under the vast starry sky.

HEIGHT: **33 ft., 49 ft., or 66 ft.**
(10 m, 15 m, or 20 m)
INTERIOR AREA: **As requested**
USE: **Sleeping under the stars**

An intimate corner for enjoying
a bubble bath at sunset.

A 360-degree view onto
a dream landscape.

The bathroom.

Dream again, daring to obtain all our desires,
so that we may one day reach the stars.

All of the photographs in this book are by **Jacques Delacroix**, with the exception of the images on the following pages:

pages 10–15 © Lars Gundersen

pages 24–27 © Maria Zhilenkova

pages 39, 51, 93, 117, 131, 151, 175, 221 © Anne-Marie Bourgeois

pages 42–45 © Maurizio Brera

pages 66–69 © Judith Edelmann

pages 88–92 © Steve Helms

pages 102–103 © Daniel Dufour

pages 188–191 © Stuart Pearce

All of the illustrations in this book are by **Daniel Dufour**, with the exception of the images on the following pages:

page 222 (top) and pages 228–229 © Ghislain André

pages 230–237 © Daï Sugasawa

I think that with this team—who can work in -22°F (-30°C) temperatures to suspend, plant, float, connect, furnish, wire, and equip to realize all of the dreams of our clients—we could work on the moon if trees existed there.

The following dream team made this book possible:

Aude Mantoux, velvet voice, velvet hands, velvet gloves.

Anne-Marie Bourgeois, gentle and a good listener.

Sonia Buchard, who won the proofreading marathon with great talent.

Valérie Gautier, who set the example.

Anne Serroy, charm, smiles, and persuasion.

Laurence Alvado, who lets nothing escape him.

Morgane Sort—what would we be without this great production manager?

Jocelyn Rigault, attentive and caring.

Hervé, a door always open.

And finally, thanks to our 450 clients and friends, who each have a desire to disconnect from the world from time to time.

Thanks to everyone for the adventure!

Alain Laurens
WWW.LA-CABANE-PERCHEE.COM
+33 4 90 75 91 40

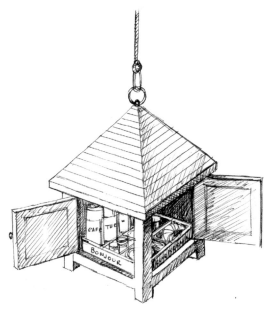

French Edition

Design and production: m87design
Text adaptation: Laurence Alvado
Editorial team: Styles

Abrams Edition

Editor: Laura Dozier
Designer: Shawn Dahl, dahlimama inc
Production Manager: Denise LaCongo

Library of Congress Control Number: 2015937589

ISBN: 978-1-4197-1974-5

Printed and bound in France by Pollina - L71956C
10 9 8 7 6 5 4 3 2 1

Abrams books are available at special discounts when purchased in quantity for premiums and promotions as well as fundraising or educational use. Special editions can also be created to specification. For details, contact specialsales@abramsbooks.com or the address below.

THE ART OF BOOKS SINCE 1949

115 West 18th Street
New York, NY 10011
www.abramsbooks.com